THE DEATHBED POET
AND OTHER POEMS

by the same author

MISERABLE LOVE POETRY & OTHER POEMS

The Deathbed Poet and Other Poems

ANTHONY WHITE

Mislove Publishing

Contents

1
THE DEATHBED POET

Comeback	5
The Deathbed Poet	6
Complaints Department	8
The Viking Funeral	9
I'm not going to talk to you differently coz you're dying	14
Aquabob	16
What It's Like	18
When I Am Dead	21
La Petite Mort	22
It Isn't Him	23
Folkestone Benches	25
They have ferried me into the viewing room	30
Funeral Party	32

You're Going To Miss Me When I'm Gone   34

2
OTHER POEMS

Hanging on to the Last of my Integrity   37

Lover's Knot   39

Pebble   40

Postcards   42

You can tell me   44

Becoming   45

Happy Families   46

Appreciating Spring   48

This is a Work of Spectacular Pointlessness   49

Derek and Catriona   51

Horace: Odes Book I Ode IX   54

Horace: Odes Book I Ode V   56

Old Neptune's Dead   58

The Man Who Cut Off His Nose   60

The Poet Goes on a Bender   62

A Seagull Shits on William Harvey   63

Self-Isolation April 2020   65

Spring Wind	70
The Ungodly Hour of the Morning	72
Under the Barrel Vault	74
Wednesdays	76
Self-Isolating On My Birthday	81
The Talking Dog	82
Three Places To Stay in Düsseldorf	84
The Badger	87
Archaeology	89
If I live long enough	92
NOTES	94
ABOUT THE AUTHOR	97

Copyright © 2023 by Anthony White

All rights reserved. No part of this book may be reproduced in any manner whatsoever without written permission except in the case of brief quotations embodied in critical articles and reviews.

First Printing, 2023

ANTHONY WHITE
The Deathbed Poet
and
Other Poems

To Kathy, whose idea this was

1

The Deathbed Poet

Somewhere in this drum of ashes
Is who I used to be.
A man scarred by a thousand lashes,
That was me.

Somewhere you will strew this dust,
But don't expect to learn
Anything of the man they burned.

Keep the urn.

Comeback

Did you see anything?
The people cried
Did you see anything
On the other side?

I saw the heavens and the heavenly host
The saints in all their glory
The angels and the archangels
Christ triumphant on his throne
And after that
Nothing

The Deathbed Poet

The deathbed poet
Reads a couplet
Softly, clearly,
Leans nearly
To the dying ear,
Unconscious of fear,
Making sure the words
Cannot be heard
By the bored,
Tired, snivelling
Bystanders welling
Up from time to time,
Reassuring each other: "It's her time".

The deathbed poet
Does not do assessments.
The poems have lines
About ancient heroes, today's headlines,

The pleasures and the anguishes of love;
Lines about sky, trees, leaves,
About dogs and neighbours,
Children, ice-cream flavours,
The undertaker's polished hat,
About this-and-that.

The deathbed poet
Does not know if
The ear so close
Hears or knows
What is meant,
Who it was who sent
This visitor, this stranger;
And the wetted sponge
Will not unlock the lips to brood
On what was not or what was understood.

It is in the tiny space between
The poet's lips and the single ear,
Held for a moment and then gone.

Complaints Department

They say I gave no comfort to her.
It is a simple misunderstanding.
They should have asked for a priest,
For palliation, painkillers;
Poetry does not promise suchlike things.

My literature makes it clear
That I do not promise comfort.
My concern is for rhythm, rhyme;
Anapaests, iambs, punctuation, semi-colons.

The Viking Funeral

i
It's the way I tell 'em
Says the fellow with the throat-beard
Whose name I have already forgotten,
Who had told me a joke I didn't understand.
(The one about asking them not to close the coffin
Until he had found his contact lens.)
Was making funeral jokes what we were here for?

The way Don Ryan was laid to rest
Is, as people say, another story.
He was fifty-eight or fifty-nine I guess
When his rotten lungs began to kill him.
Sooner or later I heard about the weird
Fantastical funeral they had planned;
Though 'planned' is wrong- they couldn't plan for toffee,

He and Bronwen (Bronwen once the singer in
   the band
And Don's lover; all too often
Ill herself and crazy)- no, they couldn't run a whelk
   stand
Or a piss-up in a brewery; but it cheered
Them to think how they'd sail him out to sea
In a burning ship- a Viking Funeral
For Don the Viking; more glorious in his death
   than in his life.

ii
When Don died a sister we'd never heard of
Appeared, established herself as next-of-kin
And had him cremated before you could say knife,
Before poor Bronwen had got herself out of bed.
What will I do? she blubbed; *he was my life;*
He was my life and now they tell me I've no rights.

The idea itself was crazy, and she so mad
I thought it just as well she had no rights.
Besides, though no-one calls it 'living-in-sin'
These days, it didn't say much for Don
That he had left poor Bronwen no more than her
   burden
Of grief. Why the heck hadn't they got wed?
They could have had one of those deathbed
   marriages-
I liked those.

But they didn't, and Don was disposed of
In that hole-and-corner way, and Bronwen
Was left weeping and wailing, like a Banshee
I suppose; not that I know what a Banshee is or
   does.
I thought that would be the last I saw of her-
A weeping woman with nothing left to live for,
Twisting a soaking hankie in her hands.

iii
The invitation came in Spring. I'd half-forgotten
   them,
For life goes on- I had plenty of others with rotten
   lungs to care for,
And the dead can take care of themselves.
But when I read *Join Us To Say Farewell*
To Don Ryan 1954-2012
This Will Be The Real Thing, The Viking Funeral
We Promised Him. Hammersmith Bridge 4pm

I cleared my diary of the living.
It was more necessary to see these Vikings.
So here I am, or there I was, listening
To throat-beard's meagre jokes, impatient
To bear witness to this spectacle,
Expecting it would add to all my likings
Something sublime, Wagnerian, grand.

That isn't true of me, you understand (it's throat-
       beard;
I've not been listening; where did this begin?)
But it's a true story all the same;
Happened to someone somewhere, lots of people;
Maybe it even happened once to you.
You must meet Reg- where is he now? - and I thought
No, it can't be true; there can't be a
    Reg The Viking.

iv
Reg carried a staff and wore a coat of midnight blue.
He had a whopper of a drinking horn slung across
       his back,
Wisps of white hair below the bald dome of his
       head.
From time to time he drank from the horn.
Reg was the leader of the pack.
Good of you to come, he said; *There won't be many
       more like this.*
There aren't so many of us left now. O- why's that?
Well, the Vikings went very PC five or six years ago.

I wondered again if this was a comedy show,
A comedy funeral for comedy Don.
Reg wiped his moustache of beer- (or was it mead?)
       froth.
Here they are he said, and there they were-
Bronwen in shocking pink with flowers in her hair,

And clutching flowers in her fists. A man in plain
    clothes
Carrying the bathtub-sized, bedecked-with-flowers
    Viking ship.

He set the ship down and we clapped and took
    snaps.
Don's picture was the sail, the rest was flowers.
And then to the water's edge, where Bronwen
    scattered flowers,
And Reg said some last words to fare him well;
And then they pushed it out on to the river,
And Reg stood with his staff, cloak billowing in the
    breeze,
And Bronwen wept and threw her last few flowers

And blew kisses and waved and called out to Don.
The ship didn't float out far.
It bobbed on the water, turned its prow
And came back to the landing-place.
Pushed out again, it returned once more.
Bronwen laughed through her tears and cried
He doesn't want to leave us.

Poor Don, poor Bronwen, poor Vikings—
None of them wants to leave us.

I'm not going to talk to you differently coz you're dying

I'm not going to talk to you differently coz you're
  dying.
I hope you are not expecting me to be
As wonderful as you are with your life-enhancing
Word for everyone, just the right amounts
Of anger and fear, and, best of all,
Using cuss words you never used before
("Why shouldn't I?" you say; "I'm fucking dying"),
Using them more, I notice, when the cheery chaplain
  comes
And leaving him more knotty-browed and thoughtful.

You've never had it so good
With your hospice care and your Radio 4 documentaries,
Not going *gently* into some good night,
But *un*gently, into who knows what-
"Yes, I'll die; but I'll die when I'm fucking ready"-
And somehow, with your plain-speaking imperturbability,
Leaving death even more of a mystery.

Aquabob

This is not about death and deathbeds, but there is a graveyard in it. The oldest bit of Folkestone is called The Bayle- an abbey was built there in the 7th century for Eanswythe, an Anglo-Saxon princess, who became St Eanswythe and the patron saint of Folkestone. One of her miracles was to give sight to a blind man. Aquabob is an old Kentish dialect word for icicle.

-It would be grand, you know, to make a legend of it,
Up there, on The Bayle, where an abbey used to sit.
There isn't enough Past here, nothing to hold on to
In times of change. But there's an epic here,
   by the sea,
A story begging to be retold
(If we could only trust the story).

There's a mistake can be made in looking back
And thinking that they must have been like us,

Those sweet, tough, virginal women
Who fed the poor and made the blind to see.
But the difference I see is that
Their souls- those damned things- had much more
 use,
The muscle of it stronger than ours today.

You'll say the legend's patently not true
But isn't that rating truth a bit too high?
Can you honestly say that you live your life like that?

It would be grand to take the path up here
Some smoky, frozen evening in December.
The child will say its spooky.
You'll trip on a tuft or slip on the icy ground
In the finger-cold,
Find yourself back in a world that is dark and cold,
A world that is dead and gone, unlike the one we have
Which is only dying.

And well might you protest that this is bathos.
We are not worthy of this place
Where grandmothers bring children to be healed.

What It's Like

Who is it lying there alive but dead,
Recognised but unrecognisable,
The same but utterly changed?
With all the powers I have I cannot make it live,
This body not quite yet a skeleton
In a hospital nightie a colour she would never have
   chosen.

Carpe diem! Carpe noctem!
The sun rises. Night must fall.
Every day there is beauty to be seen
If we but look, love to be found
If we but open our hearts.

O but I cry for all those
Who never see beauty, never feel love.

Carpe diem! Carpe noctem!
As the hour approaches, everything closes-
The banks, the shops, the doctor's office,

Restaurants and bars. We can go home now,
Retire to our beds and sleep.

O but I cry for all those
Who cannot sleep for the pain.

Carpe noctem! The clock chimes again.
Do not be afraid to go too far.
Truth lies beyond; as we arrive at
The moment of forgiveness and of being forgiven
Everything withdraws inside,
Speech is too weak to be heard,
The pulse too weak to be felt,
Eyes no longer connect,
Fingers pluck the bedspread,
Underneath the creams and powders
A faint odour of body,
The pain too weak to disturb,
The mind far gone, nowhere near
Knowing who sits at the bedside,
Too late for famous last words,
Just a bubble of spit on the lips.

Restless, plucking the bedclothes, muttering.
What is she trying to say? Something that matters?
Doctor, help! She's agitated again.
Yes, yes- we can give her something for that.

Carpe. Diem.
5 a.m.
Light but still dark,
Over but not over,

The only sound the infrequent rattling breath.
There can be a late, lucid moment,
Silly sometimes- *I could murder a plate of chips;*
But it's only a moment's fancy,
They won't be eaten,
They are hot but they soon go cold,
And then there is no sound,
The fingers are still.
What do we have to do now?
Where must we go next?
Where do we have to go now?
Who will look after us there?

When I Am Dead

When I am dead please bury my remains.
Please sing the psalm and sprinkle holy water
Before you begin the shovelling on of earth.
They are important, these rites of which I shall know
    nothing.

Afterwards, and more importantly,
The canapés and lashings of champagne.
Please use the house and not the parish hall,
And let the keynote of the day be mirth.

It might amuse you to construct a mausoleum.
You can visit, bring flowers, search your memory,
Light votive candles, close your eyes on tears,
Take pleasure in the entry in the architectural guide-

-A folly, but a fine monument, with weeping putti at
    the top
 Nothing is known of him, he was not a local man

La Petite Mort

After such happiness you long for death-
Post-coital tristesse, la petite mort-
And after that short death you long for more
And will do for as long as you have breath.

I am so happy I could die right now-
I have said this; I have heard it said-
After this short life you long for more
And then you join the dead.

It Isn't Him

i
It isn't him
My mother cried.
We stood in the Chapel of Rest
On either side
Of his stone, uncovered face.
He looks very dead
Were my small words of comfort.
I think we might have held hands and said a prayer.
We were about only ten or fifteen minutes there.

It's hardly worn
My mother said,
Pressing his winter coat on me.
I imagined its pockets housing my frozen hands.
The coat would never get used to me.
I put it with the stuff for the charity shop,
Remembering when I was a nipper,
How my hand was always in his pocket
Among the shillings and the half-a-crowns.

If I took it now
I'd fill the pockets with rocks
And drown it in the pond.
They can't blame me any more, not now.

My mother used to work in D.H.Evans.
With all her selling skills she tried
To get me to take a few of my father's ties.
Thank God she didn't get down to his small clothes.
I wouldn't be seen dead in those.

ii
If it's a broken neck you want
You're going the right way about it.
It's my father, watching me
Act the giddy goat in the playground,
The wrong way up, in fact-
Held on by my knees,
Hair brushing the concrete,
Corduroy shorts hanging down
Into my groin.
As the roundabout whirled me around
And out of his sight
It's my bloody neck! I yelled.

Folkestone Benches

There are lots of benches in Folkestone and most of them have memorial plaques fixed to them: In memory of so-and-so, Mum and Dad etc who loved sitting here looking at the sea. If you don't know Folkestone, The Leas is the clifftop promenade, where there are lots of such benches. I haven't changed the names.

The fishers unimpatient sit.
They angle in their emptied minds.
Behind, a worn-out plaque recalls
The Bailiff, dead at thirty-five.
His name was Steve, born 1965.
Happy Memories, it says; At Rest.

Memories of you Stay with us Forever
Loving Husband, Father, Grandfather
Goodnight Godbless.
I cannot tell you how they dressed

But know that once they walked their dogs,
Sat here to rest.
Now they, too, are At Rest.

An exhortation- Love Live Laugh
Beside the Water- Ved Siden Auf Hauet
Thomas, Josef, Pop – Forever In Our Hearts
Your Loving Family.
Half of my Life- a Gift of Heaven To Us
My Angel Daughter Rest In Peace
So Dearly Loved and Missed so Much.
In memory
In memory of
In loving memory
In memoriam
Farvel lille Skat, sol godt
Treasured memories
In memory of
Memoria in aeterna

We like to think of people who are dead
(Memories of you stay with us Forever).
There is the not-knowing-
Not-knowing who they were and how they talked,
What they were like.
There is only this best of them,
The happy times, the ever-love, all that is missed
    and lost.

Will be missed by family and friends
Love and miss you
Mum Nan and Greatnan

All of the folk who loved The Leas
June Ruth Fulford Muriel Trotter
Kathleen Hattie Bristow
Kenneth Charles Bristow
(Such happy Times)
Leslie Porter Mary Cleghorn
John Stuart-Bottle, Surgeon
(Justum et tenacem propositi virum)
Josephine Odile Flageollet
Constance Alice Bartlett
Marjorie Cook
Adrian 'Ginge' Petley, Alan and Maureen Petley
(Loved to stroll along The Leas and gaze
   across the Channel
Come sit here and gaze with us for a while)

For all the happy times
Much loved and remembered by all
A Friend to All
Loved by All
Adored by All
Always Remembered
Always in our Thoughts

Together again
My one and only love for 67 years
Loved and missed every day
'Til we meet again, George

Dulcis Pro Patria Labor
In ever-loving memory of our dear parents
Albert John
Valerie Evelyn
Who were married in this town in 1947
They dreamed their dreams and taught us to follow
    ours

To sit with people who have died-
my wife, our mutti-
On sunny days, at Whitsuntide-
Edith Anna, Brakel, Westphalia-
Eating ice-cream side by side-
The most Beautiful mum, nana and sister
May you dance my darling dance
With the angels in the vibration of love

In memory of
In loving memory
In memoriam
Farvel lille skat, sol godt
Treasured memories
In memory of
Memoria in aeterna

They have ferried me into the viewing room

They have ferried me into the viewing room.
I shan't complain; it's only temporary;
And the chaplain is by in case of my breaking down.

The mortician has finished me off lovely.
My eyes are closed, the laugh wiped from my face,
My forehead and my cheeks undrawn with lines.

(Why couldn't I have looked like this in life?)

The children will come soon (or some of them;
This is not everyone's cup of tea).
They'll come when they've finished playing
   in the park-

For I see them as they were, whirling the roundabout
As fast as it would go, pushing the swings
As high, not caring a jot for my worry.

They'll tell me it was one of the others' fault
They're crying, when they come in and show me
Their blackened elbows and grazed knees.

I can't care any more. It's their turn now to live.

Funeral Party

After my mother died,
My father having gone ten years before,
About a hundred people came to the funeral,
A hundred mourners to scatter earth
And lay down wreaths above her.
Yes, there were about a hundred people,
Some of them old friends and neighbours, but mostly
Family- extended family, cousins, third-cousins
   and so on,
People of all ages from ninety years to nine weeks,
Most of whom found a way to offer their sincere
Whatsits and ask me how I was feeling;
Most of them, after a bit of the emotional stuff,
Leaning towards practical matters,
What will you do with the house? and so on
(The house having been as famous as my parents).

After the first drink and a go at the buffet lunch
It became a common theme
That we had mourned in church and at the burial

And now was the time to celebrate our much-loved
Much-missed etcetera, who would want us
To enjoy ourselves
Not cry.

When my mother died I thought
That's it then; I'm free at last,
And then about a hundred people,
Most of them family,
Came for the funeral party.

I thought they would never go.

You're Going To Miss Me When I'm Gone

I suppose you'll want some music at my funeral.
Well do what you like- I won't be there.
You'll Never Walk Alone. I Will Survive.
Ye Gods! The feelings won't be mutual.

But let me just have a whisper in your ear
Coz while I'm still here I can't be neutral.
Whatever it is you think I'd want to hear
You're wrong.
You *never* listened while I was
Alive.

2

Other Poems

Hanging on to the Last of my Integrity

At the Saturday matinees, black was what
  the bad guys wore,
But the sheriff was quicker on the draw–
Put your hands up! Drop your guns to the floor!
Was the kind of morality play we saw.
Then, evil had its proper place; the law
Was stronger (better-looking, too). The War
Was won by Englishmen with strong jaws,
Clean-cut chaps who never even swore.
What blood there was was Kensington Gore.
O gimme more, I thought, *Give Me More*.

My girlfriend's cat licking blood from its paw
Was real-er, a taste of life-in-the-raw,
But it wasn't what we were looking for.
The dance of the seven veils with the girl next door,

Things my sister kept in her private drawer,
The music no one else liked, the clothes we wore,
The death squads in Vietnam and El Salvador,
Mao's Little Red Book, Simone de Beauvoir,
These things unsoftened us, got us ready for
Settlement- work and wages, children, a labrador.
O gimme more, I thought, *Give Me More.*

The way we live now grew from those seeds
   and spores.
The movies aren't black and white anymore.
We've taken holidays in the Azores,
Eaten tofu burgers, drunk whisky galore.
All the pieces fitted in the jigsaw.
Now it's like somebody took a chainsaw
To all that, as if the house was built of straw.
A hard rain sluices clean the concrete floor,
Leaving no trace of what was there before.
The iron fist in the velvet claw,
The raw recruits, the conscripts, the herbivores,
The true allegiants staunch and sure,
The vaccine junkies hot for war.
Listen! Watch! The gunboats mass offshore.
Gimme more. Gimme more. Give me more.

Lover's Knot

By the same token the different body
In the same bed in the same bedsit
Gave different pleasures in the same positions
For the same short time, with the same urgings,
The same things moaned and said.
I would have kept returning,
To meet new tenants, new lodgers,
Through the same entrance and exit-
Different pleasures in the same conditions-
All spoiled when the landlord put in a new bed.

Pebble

Who knows what might depend on my recording this?
That words might fail me goes without saying,
But who knows what or who in this dead end of night,
Might escape me, scarper without paying,
If I write out no receipt.

I could retreat into dreams, but they can't be relied on-
A blank cheque you handed to a stranger-
They overlook too much, their beams so bright
A furious waking breaks the calmness of sleep.
A dream is a promise to pay that is never kept.

Therefore the actuality's the thing, *this* stone in *this* street,
A nothing-worth-bothering-about, and yet
Acknowledgement seems right for every piece of the earth,
A pebble's mettle as vital a quality
As the value of a fifty-pound note.

The sun has moved around to kiss the pebble.
They use a language long lost to us, but which we will
 recover
As we journey from rebellion to infinity,
Through with worship, that waste of Time, itself a
 waste,
Balancing gain and loss, ever counting costs.

Postcards

The postcards take up little space.
White-tacked to the 'fridge they
Cover its off-putting white face
With a sort of incomplete art history-
Mostly the acknowledged greats-
Mixed with a sort of incomplete world tour,
Capri, Tiananmen Square,
Battlefields of the First World War,
Butlin's Minehead, Kazakhstan World Fair,
Wroslaw, Egypt, The United States.

Then, juxtaposed with Warhol's Marilyn,
A Bauhaus armchair, Rembrandt's wife,
Hiroshi Sato Mannequins,
A William Nicholson Still Life.

The transport links are good here
And it doesn't take me long
To reach the hallway where are
Disneyland, Hong Kong,

Dublin's (Joyce's) Sandymount Strand,
The Nagasaki Bullet Train,
Grand Canyon, Berlin Zoo,
J.M.Turner's *Clouds and Rain*,
Barbados, Tangier (general view),
Several other Disneylands.

Next to these a Botticelli sits
By Tokyo, the spires of Chartres,
A bowler-hatted fellow of Magritte's,
All kinds of 4-by-6-inch art,
The world from Leicester Square to Newfoundland.

These are mementos of other people's lives,
Their beaten and unbeaten tracks,
Their favourite beaches, hotels, dives,
Their Guggenheim, *their* Louvre, *their* Prado,
Their yearly search for El Dorado.
It's years since I read what's written on their backs.

You can tell me

You can tell me.
I've heard it all before.
It's the same old story
But you are different.
I can listen.
I can simply be.

You can tell me.
I know it's baloney
But the same is true
Of Creon and Antigone,
Finnegan, Daedalus, Bloom.
You'll see.

You can tell me.
I will hoard it in my heart
And forget it all.
I am the one hurt,
At your beck and call,
No win, no fee.

Becoming

Becoming, when they removed the brace from her
 teeth,
A woman, she smiled without reserve,
And never let me see what lay beneath
The dazzling beauty that I thought meant love.

Happy Families

This is Mr. Butcher, the candlestick-maker
And here's Mrs. Baker, the wife of the butcher
And here's Master Candle, the son of the baker
And here is Miss Stick, who is somebody's sister

And here is Miss Butcher, the candlestick-maker's daughter
And here's Mr. Baker, the husband of the wife of the butcher
And here's Mrs Candle, the mother of the son of the baker
And here's Master Stick, who is somebody's brother

And that Mr. Butcher says Who makes the candles?
And that Mrs. Baker says Who still eats meat?
And that Master Candle says Stop making your own bread!
And Miss Stick says O! When will someone want to share my bed?

The butcher the baker the candlestick-maker
Have seen their fortunes in the cards.
Happy Families, they read, though their
    businesses are bust.
Miss Stick says Things must get better, O! surely they
    must.

Appreciating Spring

Is it wrong to turn away from the important things
To admire the birds and blossoms that come back in
   Spring?
While the tanks move and the lies stream from the
   screens,
To look up at the rooftops where light gleams
And the sun shines in a clear blue sky
Down at the little flowers? Ask not why,
On the bridge across the stream, two lovers
Stand below two free, ecstatic doves.

This is a Work of Spectacular Pointlessness

So many things have happened since I saw you last.
Largesse of Spring has happily returned-
Traveller's Joy, Meadowsweet and, best of all,
Bluebells ring out new beginnings.

Bringing also an end, as in our last school year,
When, yearning to put away childish things,
There came to us the happy thought
That soon we would never again have to open Chaucer,
Had survived The War of the Spanish Succession.

Celebrate too the end of the wearing of uniforms.
Following the timetable of arrivals and departures
We urged on ourselves adulthood-
Happiness, hope, liberty, life-long friendships.

It's a melancholy business, revisiting the past,
Trying to sort the remembered from the real.
You popped into my head out of nowhere,
Wearing the only togs I'd ever seen you in;
Still 18, your face as bright as a spring flower,

Ordinarily beautiful, and not someone I knew,
Not then or since. Still, I hope you had a good one,
Once you got out of that uniform.
If I knew where you lived, I'd send you daffodils.

Derek and Catriona

When Catriona, the contrabassoonist in the Barra and Benbecula Community Orchestra,
And Derek, the drummer in *Dark Werewolf*, Hayling Island's premier death metal band ('Weddings 'r' Us'),
Met and fell in love,
It was a match made in Heaven-
Too far apart to often meet, and with too many artistic differences to dare to talk,
They got on like a house on fire,
Not that they had a house to be on fire.

A few times a year
They stayed together in Glasgow at the Euro Hostel (£10 a night at time of writing).
They never explored Glasgow, but Catriona explored Derek's body, which was covered all over with hair, and which was adorned with a single erogenous

piercing, and with a dozen rings on his fingers; while Derek marvelled that he should find himself in love with, as well as find himself loved by, this fresh-faced, apple-cheeked, softly-spoken, Outer Hebridean sex machine.

"Can you get electric contrabassoons?" he would tease her. "Perhaps Dark Werewolf should have one".
Catriona would pause momentarily in toying with Derek's piercing to say "Do you think that would put Dark Werewolf a cut above other death metal bands, or would your fans see it as a betrayal of your artistic integrity?"
"And what if you", Derek was quick to come back, "went electric? Would the Barra and Benbecula band have your guts for garters?"

After breakfast, which was five items for £4.50, of which Derek had four (sausage sandwich, beans, poached egg and coffee), and Catriona had one (fruit tea), they would say goodbye at the station.
Catriona would catch the train that took her to Oban, from where the CalMac ferry took four hours and fifty minutes to deliver her to Barra;
While Derek went on a National Express coach, which took ten hours and fifty minutes, changing at Birmingham, to reach London, where he would stay with his brother for a night before returning to Hayling Island.

They went on like this for seven years, until one day
Catriona texted Derek to say: *I'm getting married.
Bit of a coincidence actually, as he too is a
percussionist. His name is Angus. It's been great kiss
kiss smiley face teary face.*
Derek went up and played his drums for a while, very
loudly, after which he texted her back:
*Good luck. It's been nice knowing you.
Would you like us to play at your wedding?*

Horace: Odes Book I Ode IX

You see how white with snow the Malvern Hills are
How the trees and the woods can hardly bear the load
How slick with dangerous ice the roads appear
And the River Severn swollen to the brim

Then throw another log on the flaming fireplace
Abandon the crazy idea of leaving for home
Pull the cork from that bottle of Spanish wine
Come and sit down and talk, my dear young friend

As for the rest, leave it to the gods, for
As soon as they have calmed the winds
And the roiling waters, your beloved ash
And cherry trees will no longer be in danger

Why worry what tomorrow has in store
How many years Dame Fortune will grant you?
For now, neglect not in your youth the dance
And the feeling in your heart for sweet love

Tomorrow seek out again the trysting-places
Somewhere will be that laughing girl, the one
Who mocks you, but, when you look upset,
Grabs your arm and whispers *Don't go yet*

Horace: Odes Book I Ode V

O Poppy! What toned boy is this, drenched in
   aphrodisiac
Perfumes, who lies on top of you in the garden nook?
For whom have you shaken your golden locks
Free, let everything hang out?

Poor thing! How he will complain of women's fickle
Fancies, and of gods, and marvel instead
At the turbulent sea
And the black oncoming storm,

Who now shags you, missionary style,
Fondly thinking you pure and his alone,
Imagining you will always be like this,
Unsullied by love's ups and downs.

Poor fool! mistaking your flirtation for devotion.
Not that I care- I have hung up my diving gear
As a thanksgiving offering to the god
Of that rocky sea.

Old Neptune's Dead

Otters almost disappeared from England in the 1970s after pesticides routinely used for decades had brought their numbers to near extinction levels. Now many of those chemicals have been banned and the creatures are present again in rivers across England. The first I knew of this was when I read that otters had been seen again in Cambridgeshire. (In 2011, two otters were spotted in Kent, signalling their return to every English county.)

Old Neptune's dead, who raised the walls of Troy,
And Cupid's lethal arrows are but toys.
There is no Robin Hood to feed the poor,
No poets hymn the ecstasies of war.
St George, who killed the dragon in his prime,
Is a refuge for scoundrel-patriots in our time.
Though Arthur will not come again this year,
The otters have returned to Cambridgeshire.

Great Pan is dead, the temple fires are out,
And Achilles is bedridden with gout.
Heroes we worshipped once have feet of clay,
And every mangy dog must have its day.
No matter, be of good heart, good cheer.
The otters have returned to Cambridgeshire.

The Man Who Cut Off His Nose

He cut off his nose to spite his face
Then saw that he needed to fill the space
Where his nose used to be
He tried on a mask but it wouldn't grip
It would have sat on his nose's tip
But he had no nose, so he had no tip
And the mask *would* slip

He cut off his nose to spite his face
But his face fought back to spite the place
Where his nose used to be
It left a trace above his lip
Where the mask hung on that had no grip
It hung on his lip and it gave him gyp
For the mask *would* slip

He cut off his nose to spite his face
But thought the space was lacking grace

Where his nose used to be
So he told himself to get a grip
And he pulled out his knife and cut off the lip
Where the mask had hung that gave him gyp
Then the other lip

He cut off his nose to spite his face
Sure he was helping the human race
Who still had eyes to see
But he worried about the eyes that were left
Above the cleft of his sliced-off nose
So he took his knife and he struck a pose
And he said *Here Goes*

And he cut out the eyes to spite the space
Where his nose and lips and mask used to be.
The last step of all is to cut out his brains
The brains that keep on telling him he
Should have left the nose and the nose's tip
And the eyes and the upper and lower lip
So he rolls back his scalp with his fingertips.
It opens as easy as a zip.

The Poet Goes on a Bender

The wife had always dreaded Fielding's coming.
It meant three days and nights of bacchanal,
Boozing with the old pals, night-town slumming,
Drinking not eating, falling in the canal,
Then ringing her from somewhere like Blackheath-
I'm stranded, will you come and pick me up,
I'm out of money, can't find my teeth,
Be a darling, little buttercup.

And from the imagination of the home
The wife would start the car and rescue him.
Poor poet, weak as an unarmed man,
She the wife-muse-lover, number one fan.
After Fielding's going her man would sleep-
For a week, in his clothes, piss the bed-
While she would quietly clean the house and weep,
And think what, when he woke, could not be said.

A Seagull Shits on William Harvey

I feel comfortable in my skin these days,
Now the mad teenage years of living on
Nothing but chips and ice-cream, washing it down
With a lap at the cider-vomit of the town's
Youth problem, have gone.

I single out William Harvey to praise
For *De Motu Cordis et Sanguinis*.
Extraordinary Physician to King James,
The jurat's son, though sceptical of witches,
Proved himself worthy

Of *his* life, the motion of *his* heart and blood,
And, in a way, showed the cider-puking low life
No less like those of superior blood.
That's worth a statue, quincentennial fame-
They were worth it, weren't they?

So when you see the anointment of dried crud
That decorates Harvey's head and shoulders,
Don't turn up your nose, but use your loaf-
It is I, now much wiser and much older,
Who offers *this* tribute to *his* natural philosophy-

The circulation of shit on the human body.

Self-Isolation
April 2020

In April 2020, we were all intending to do wonderful things while we were locked down- learn to play the piano, speak Japanese, make sourdough bread etc. That's what was on my mind when I wrote this.

It is written in verses of 16 lines, a form which has no name (a sonnet has 14 lines, but after that you're on your own), so I have come up with the word deca-existich. I know- it is not an attractive word but is the best I can do. This is a long poem of six deca-existichs.

Curdled in this exciting new kitchen machine
Are leftovers of pearls,
Old Masters, benzedrine,
Odds and ends of worlds
Beyond their age of wealth,

Of usefulness and status,
Of health, inheritance; the zealous
Self-expansion become flatus
Perfumed and provoking,
All the tensions of growth and decay
Relaxing first then choking.
Watching the blender destroy
These ingredients, I adore
Colours the like of which
I've never seen before,
But I fear this sauce will turn out much too rich.

Someway though I have to break up the morning
Or else it goes on for much too very long
And I find myself yawning,
Feeling good-for-nothing and unstrung,
Almost wishing the day were ended
Before it has begun.
We have to make a life and not pretend it,
And so I put my apron on,
The one that says *Real Men Wear Aprons*,
And create these novel recipes,
Like one of those old matrons
Of an ancient peasantry.
I am learning how to smile in my sleep,
Write in trochaic pentameters,
'Til the man with feet of brass comes in his jeep
With a sword in his mouth and a parcel from Amazon.

Years ago- I mean many years-
I set my face against death,
Raised my flag and gave three cheers
For life and being free and for progress.
That was too mad, so I set my face against life
And began to merely pass the time,
Sitting in coffee shops with free wi-fi,
Watched Narcissus perform his comic mime
In studio theatres. I talked to him once.
He told me what it's like to fail in Hollywood,
How it's like the death of romance,
How he returned to England like Sir Walter Raleigh
    would
With traveller's tales of Venice Beach,
The muscle-bound women who taught him how to jog
(Their teeth as white as mirrors), how to eat a peach,
Chipotle ketchup, corn dogs.

This is exactly how it happened.
If I can put it this way-
From the teacher we gave apples
To the one we nicknamed Nuts-in-May,
The one I mocked along with all the others
While craving his respect
(I was not the one who took the gloves off).
I learned my Shakespeare, Wordsworth, passed the
    tests,
And only when my passions turned to love
Did I meet someone who could look me in the face

To say with passion of her own: "My God! Those
   gloves!"
I stopped her mouth with kisses for a space
Then changed my style.
I am pulling a few dead languages out of the fire
And may try some choriambs, dactyls;
Accompany myself on the lyre.

So much for that; it's getting on for midnight
(All day I should have had better things to do),
The sky a uniform dark grey, the street lights
Marring the precision of its hue.
First and last the credulous guillemots
Whose offspring leap from cliffs before they can fly.
The Foolish Guillemots have learned how to be silly,
How not to fly yet not to die.
Of all the things I could do now-
Grow lettuce on my balcony, cook and sew,
Read a yard or two of highbrow
Books, learn to play the piano-
For whom? becomes the unbegging question.
Those gawky gulls surprise me every time-
They don't live here; I've never seen one,
And yet they keep on landing on my rhymes.

In the beginning- *initium*- we create,
Simply by beginning alter the world.
We splash into the sea, we will not wait
To be taught, to be told.

You can't expect every moment to be like that!
You say; and so say I.
We must be born again, in lean years and in fat.
Every time we say goodbye
I live a little. I am learning to make up my mind
Never to make up my mind- at last
A proposition I can get my head around.
The solitude goes by too fast.
Every moment's a thing I learn anew.
Should we not nurture what's good? Get rid of what's
　　gone to seed?
Well...no. I am creating what's over, too.
Until I've done that, there's nothing to do but read.

Spring Wind

Even before spring we had been warned
Not to go outdoors unless we must.
"The winds will storm the city like a war.
No one will hear you speak against its roar.
The winds are fit to bust.
Stay calm, stay safe, stay warm."

This is my chanson de geste, the song of my deeds.
While the wind blew like truth
At the trees, I dressed as in widow's weeds
To mourn, with the wind as my muse,
To tell on my prayer beads
Where the wind's destruction leads.

And even when the solstice of my heart
Felt the chill,
Even when they warned that war might start,
The sun stand still,
The wind, not-visible, not-speaking, blew to impart
The news you don't see on the weather chart.

Even then I refused to give up hope.
I watched the wind wrestle the trees.
Some stood, some of the weak ones dropped.
They used to tell me speech was free
But now they have stopped.
They will not listen until all trees are lopped.

(*chanson de geste-* song of heroic deeds)

The Ungodly Hour of the Morning

...comes later now than then.
When my mother hissed from the top of the stairs
"I told you to be home by ten
I've been worried sick", I didn't think I cared.
Was ten a godly hour and midnight not?
I never asked. I was red rag to a bull enough
Without probing that inflammatory spot.
Instead, I shrugged off my guise as a young tough,
Said "Sorry Mum, I won't do it again".
I said that every time I caused her pain;
Every time I put the door back on the chain.

These days it comes between three and four.
My mum's no longer here to put me straight,
Kiss my forehead, tell me not to fret.
Ungodly, a ridiculous metaphor
It was then, it just made me want to laugh;
It is now, it really doesn't help.

I've discovered *I* can be worried sick as well.
When I was sixteen I thought my mother daft,
She on the landing, I at the front door;
Those summit meetings during our Cold War.
Fifty years on, I wish I'd loved her more.

Under the Barrel Vault

Under the barrel vault and the sanctuary lamp
And the life-size crucifix, the women sweep and polish
Until you can see your face in the altar rails.
None of them are young.

At this time they are masked and gloved.
Neither do they fail to put back the signs that list
    all the precautions
Nor to make sure the sanitary liquids
('Miracle' brand?) are where they should be.

They sweep behind the orange food-bank tubs,
Clean the wax from the votive candle stand.
Perhaps they half-hope nobody will come
And spoil it all again.

This is a kind of faith that has endured.
They leave it looking like a Dutch painting
From another century,
Tenebrous, spotless, empty,
Ready for the entry of the visitants,
The ones who come but once a year,
As well as the old faithfuls, those
Whose heart skips a beat when the bells are rung.

Wednesdays

Of late the need to meet as if at first-
Recognition, of course, taking its place,
The easy bits of where you like to sit,
What sort of coffee, whose turn it is to pay;
Ask about the family, naturally-
And then to start afresh, with a true wish
To be easy with you like a friend;
Forgiveness- though you tell me there's no need-
Aching to take place, and after that,
Forget.

Wednesday was always Corin's day in town.
He would come down from the sheepfold in his suit,
Jingling the change in his trouser pocket,
Hopeful of good stories and company.
Over Spenser's Mound and past the Old Forge,
Into the cowprints of Jamlyn's Acre,
Over the stile, across the Beechwood Road,
Under the railway bridge, past Lovers' Lane,

All the way his shoes fall into place,
A thousand trips like this.

Along the way he improvises
A little song to hum as he tramps downhill:
"When the last of a people is gone
When the last son without child
And the last daughter without child
Have said the last syllables
Of a dead language..."

In the market he buys cherries and loose apples.
"How's the love-life, Corin?" winks the stall-holder,
And Corin tilts his free hand, gently,
As if to say 'It's so-so', or 'in the balance'.
Palmed, though, is another answer, something like
"I remember having a love-life; there was Phoebe,
The shepherdess, though finally she would not have
    me."

Crowded around their table in the pub
His different mates, the jumpered sculptors,
Painters and poets who lap their flat beer
And argue and laugh, free for a while of their art.
"I heard it", says Greg, "on the wireless,
The B-B-C! No listen, get this:
'An icon of the first and utter water'.
It's true; on the B-B-effing-C!"
And they laugh and get to talking about icons

And then heroes and then their own heroes
And Seamus starts on about Billy the Kid
And Barbara shouts him down: "Billy the Kid!-
A juvenile delinquent with a horse!"
And Seamus, his own man, quietly protests:
"You must take into account that then,
When I was a schoolboy, The West-
America!- was a faraway place,
A distant land with no landmarks or milestones.
Billy was young with a black hat and a gun
Slung on his hip- what's not to like?"

"Hey, Corin, man, the voice of reason-
Billy the Kid- hero or villain?"
Corin tilts the well-used hand again,
Says "Well, you know...", tilts it the other way.
The table roars with laughter and they chorus:
"On the one hand that, on the other, this.
Good old Corin. Drink up; what's your poison?"
He protests- "No, listen now, it's my shout",
But is overruled- "Your time will come".

Struck as always by the ordinariness
Of the artists, their scruffy hair and clothes-
All but Barbara, who looks as though she's dressed by
    Vogue-
The silly things they laugh about off-duty-
Corin is also struck, again as always,
At the sudden change when, on their fourth drink

And halfway through eating their shepherd's pie,
They become impassioned about art,
Barbara enraged today about a man
Called Crick, who "paints with both feet in his mouth-
It's an old hat he makes look like a pisspot".
Jonathan, the oldest of them, laughs and says
"Ah now, he's got something though, your man",
And Greg pipes up "Yes, he's got that talent we don't have-
He makes money", and they all laugh together,
Fit to beat the band.

He wishes he could buy their drinks; he feels
For their poorness, and he can afford it.
What's more, the fun they give is worth twice the price,
But no- they'd be insulted if he tried.
He wonders why they never talk of love.
You'd think they would, though it occurs to him
There's no parallel in the plastic arts
To the love poem, love song. Funny that.

One of the writers, a handsome boy called Matt
Is slagging off the ManBooker shortlist.
"You see Cluck's got on it again? Ye Gods!
Cluck, whose artistic credo seems to be
That a story must have a beginning,
A beginning, a middle and an end!"
Corin pipes up: "Wouldn't this be better-

Start with the end, so we know where we stand?"
He means it; he's not trying to be smart,
But Matt won't have it, and he puts him straight-
"O, that's all been done; everything has been done".
So Barbara puts an arm around his neck,
Says "Cheer up chuck, your time will surely come".

It looks as though they might go on all day
But sometime someone says "That's it for me",
And up they sup and stagger to their feet.
They kiss and embrace, shake hands with Corin.
They'll sleep it off, get up tomorrow, work.
"Corin; good man; thanks fer'; good to see you."
" 'Til next week, then." Corin says: "If we're spared".

He picks up his fruit, dusts a hand down his suit,
And goes again, clumsy over the stile,
Then glad to be back in his distant land,
The fields he used to farm. Too pissed to whistle,
He quavers a song in time with the tramps of his feet-
"*I live in a house on a hill. The dog*
Has died and I will not have another.
This is the house where Phoebe might have lived,
But she would not have me.
Since thou canst talk of love so well,
I'll endure."

Self-Isolating On My Birthday

Alone and attic'd,
As I always knew I'd end up-
Not with that pneumatic blonde
I could have paid the agency to send up,
Nor with a scrum of friends
Drinking themselves ecstatic,
Nor with a loving family in attendance
(Who think me geriatric
When I dandle the latest grandchild on my knee)-
No, this time it's only me,
Halfway through a bottle of Grand Cru '93,
Playing loud music very loud,
Still imagining I stand out from the crowd,
And, astonishingly, happy.

The Talking Dog

I wish I hadn't bought this dog that talks.
Who was that lady I saw you with last night?
He growls and I say
That was no lady that was my wife
And he says
Don't be funny buster; take me for a walk.

Once I could drink and sleep where I liked,
Wake up in some strange hotel room.
Now I have to get back to the dog,
Who looks at me and says
Don't be hurrying too fast to your tomb,
And I say
Leave me alone; tonight I need to sleep like a log.

But the dog wants food so I take him out
To the dog-friendly restaurant
Where he asks
For the wine list and the à la carte

And chats to the sommelier
And I say
Nothing over twenty pounds! and he pouts.

All the way home he sings (*Polly-wolly-doodle-all-the-day*).
He poos against my next-door neighbour's car,
Taunts me and says
Whatcha gonna do about it? Call the Neighbourhood Watch?
Well, the dog was pissed and I was pissed
And we stagger on, me fumbling with the poo-bag tie
And I say
Any more of this and you're for the chop.

Then I tripped and fell and landed on my wrist.
The poo-bag slipped from my hand, the street became a bog.
I woke in the morning to find the dog didn't exist.
Of course, I thought, as the wheels turned and the cogs-
There's no such thing as a talking dog.

Three Places To Stay in Düsseldorf

The Hotel Heinrich Heine is in the Königsallee,
Germany's most famous and iconic fashion boulevard.
Its name and décor are a tribute to the poet Heine
And Romantic Poetry-style chic runs throughout.
Heine was destitute when he died
And could not have afforded to stay here.
A charming novelty is the availability of young drama students
Who will recite Heine to you in your room-
Just ask at reception.
(Note: they don't read only the sad ones!)

From- 80 euros a night

What did you go out to see- they that wear soft raiment?
They will take yours and your lover's payment.
Morte! Baci! Iconica!

The Hotel Death Star Düsseldorf is
The most iconic hotel in Germany.
It was on the roof of the Death Star
(Then known as The Night Rendezvous Hotel)
That the poet Sauman Wegg shot himself
And toppled over the balustrade to his death
Twenty stories below.
It is not known if the shot killed him or the fall.
Now a historic site of rock 'n' roll debauchery,
Each room contains a Marshall amp
And guitars can be borrowed for free from reception.
(Note: the sound-proofing is excellent)

From: 90 euros a night

Morte! Baci! Iconica!
Their raiment white as snow

The Hat of Blood is a
140-room contemporary hotel
15 minutes from Düsseldorf airport and
Close to the old town.
Try its iconic honeymoon suite
With its double jacuzzi bath-
Truly decadent!

This is the perfect spot to explore
The thriving nightlife around Ratinger Strasse.
It has a bar and outside terrace
And there is even
A library.

From: 95 euros a night

Iconica! Baci! Morte!
I have come to wash myself in the Rhine

The Badger

As I walked down this hill towards this road,
Like one without a care in all the world,
I stopped and looked, then on I strode
In wonder there was nothing to be seen or heard.

As far as my ears could hear or eyes could see
There was nothing moving in all the world;
No birds, no folk, no creature besides me.
I went over the stile to the metalled road.

The road was as unpeopled as the path
Until I turned the bend towards the town
And saw, blocking the way, Death
In the shape of a badger, lying still as any stone.

A dead badger, and nothing else around,
Decaying in the middle of the road,
An obstruction to human traffic, food
For smaller creatures picking at its wound.

Its stale blood dirtied the tarmac where it had run.
I couldn't see its eyes, only the belt
Of slack muscle in its lustreless black pelt;
Flies buzzing around it, catching the sun.

It was a phoney summer; I'd been expecting rain.
The corpse was there all week in the same spot.
I walked around it, cars swerved around it
Without slowing, that heap of slow ruin.

On my return, I climbed over the stile
Back up the quiet hill about a mile
To the isolated cottage. It was a quiet time,
But I'd something to tell my friends about back home.

Archaeology

Beyond the swimmers, far beyond,
Until you're out of reach of their
Pretend reluctance, shrieks of fear-
Those simple pleasures you abscond;

Beyond the sea lanes, far beyond
The quinqueremes of Nineveh,
The unbound wide Sargasso sea,
The topless towers of Trebizond;

Beyond all this, the emptiness,
The silence where you seek to find
Histories hidden in the brine,
Hidden for scores of centuries.

You hope the sea gods favour your approach.
Why should they not?- you come in peace.
No magic Ring or Golden Fleece,
Nor power nor riches guide your search.

You're out-of-bounds, though, wanderer.
You're on your own, out of your depth,
Half-drown when you open your mouth for breath
Or to sing the wild blue yonder,
Outside the gulf between your dreams
And the realities you live with-
The fog, the legend and the myth,
Wild words writ by unknown names.

The waves collapse the light and tease you-
As soon as it's caught your eye it's gone.
And yet the colours of the sun
In that fleeting moment please you.

Find out the truth or die's your credo.
The fire is cast into the sea.
The sea piles wreckage on the carefree
Souls who throng the sun-blessed lido.

Under the wreckage and the dead
The tales of old you came here for.
The sea has laid them at your door
Unfinished, incomplete, unread.

Yeh yeh- you hear the mermaids singing.
It's what the fall of Rome was like-
A sudden violent final strike-
And here you reach your last beginning.

You fly, a bird now, back to the fray,
Dump your fuel- an old seagull joke
You can't resist- but they're not provoked,
The fabulous beau monde. They're miles away.

If I live long enough

If I live long enough
I'll walk these streets
And find not one inhabitant
I recognise or know
I shall look up and see
No curtains that once
Flapped gaily at me
In a spring breeze
I'll step up to the doors
And find no names
Beside the call-bells
That used to quicken my heart
No bar or café window
From which I used to gaze
Will be called the same
Nor have those friendly owners

And when I turn the corner
Go uphill past the lych gate into the churchyard
I'll find the names on gravestones
Weathered away
Impossible to read

NOTES

Folkestone Benches. 'Justum et tenacem propositi virum' means 'a man upright and firm of purpose'. The phrase begins one of Horace's Odes- Book III Ode III (*"The just man, firm of purpose, cannot be shaken in his rocklike soul, by the heat of fellow citizens clamouring for what is wrong, nor by the presence of a threatening tyrant."*). 'Dulcis Pro Patria Labor' means 'It is sweet to work for your country'. (Sounds better in Latin, I think.)

Appreciating Spring. The two lovers referred to are those in the story that you see on willow pattern plates. The daughter of a powerful Mandarin falls in love with a lowly clerk. The Mandarin is furious when he discovers this, banishes the clerk, builds a wall around the palace, and arranges for his daughter to marry a wealthy duke. The lovers manage to escape (across the bridge) but the Mandarin finds out where they are and sends his soldiers to kill them. The gods take pity on the lovers and turn their souls into doves, to fly together forever.

Horace. Horace (65-8 BC) has been more frequently translated into English than any other classical poet, and these are two efforts of my own. They are somewhat free (Horace didn't write about the Malvern Hills and the River Severn, for example) but I have tried to capture the meaning and the spirit of the originals.

A Seagull Shits on William Harvey. William Harvey is Folkestone's most famous son. Born in 1578, the son of a jurat (magistrate), he was the first to describe, in *Exercitatio Anatomica de Motu Cordis et Sanguinis in Animalibus* (Anatomical Exercise on the Motion of the Heart and Blood in Animals), the circulation of blood in the human body. In 1618 he was appointed 'Physician Extraordinary' to King James I and lived during the European witch hunt. He was involved in one of the cases, in 1634, and had to examine four women accused of witchcraft. At a time when belief in witches was commonplace and to deny their existence was heresy, it would have been very easy to interpret any suspicious behaviour or mark on the body as positive evidence of witchcraft. It is much to Harvey's credit that he treated the case with an open mind and was willing to consider scientific explanations of the evidence allegedly showing witchcraft. The alleged witches were found to be innocent.

The statue of William Harvey is unfortunate in that it attracts seagulls, and his head and shoulders are usually covered in seagull poo. In this poem I have, however, tried to see things from the seagull's point of view.

ABOUT THE AUTHOR

Anthony White is a spoken-word poet. Born in London in 1954, for most of his working life he was a nurse. Now retired, he lives in Folkestone (Kent, UK), where he writes and performs his work, mostly with Poets' Corner Folkestone, of which he is a founding member. He has also performed solo shows at Faversham Fringe Festival, and *The Deathbed Poet* was one of these. Anthony has now revised this for publication, and has added a miscellany of other poems written between 2015 and 2022.

His first collection, *Miserable Love Poetry and Other Poems*, was published in 2022.

www.ingramcontent.com/pod-product-compliance
Lightning Source LLC
Chambersburg PA
CBHW031127080526
44587CB00011B/1145